CULTURE IN ACTION

# Contortionists and Cannons

## An Acrobatic Look at the Circus

Marc Nobleman

Raintree is an imprint of Capstone Global Library Limited,
a company incorporated in England and Wales having its
registered office at 7 Pilgrim Street, London, EC4V 6LB
– Registered company number: 6695582

Text © Capstone Global Library Limited 2011
First published in hardback in 2011
The moral rights of the proprietor have been asserted.

Edited by Louise Galpine, Megan Cotugno, and Abby Colich
Designed by Ryan Frieson
Original illustrations © Capstone Global Library Ltd
Illustrated by Cavedweller Studio, Randy Schirz
Picture research by Liz Alexander
Originated by Capstone Global Library Ltd
Printed in China by China Translation & Printing
   Services Ltd

ISBN 978 1 40621 698 1
15 14 13 12 11 10
10 9 8 7 6 5 4 3 2 1

**British Library Cataloguing in Publication Data**
Nobleman, Marc Tyler
Contortionists and cannons: An acrobatic look at the circus.
– (Culture in action)
791.3'4-dc22
A full catalogue record for this book is available from the
British Library.

**Acknowledgements**
We would like to thank the following for permission to
reproduce photographs: We would like to thank the following
for permission to reproduce photographs: Alamy pp. **4** (©
Ambient Images Inc.), **6** (© North Wind Picture Archives);
Corbis pp. **7** (© Historical Picture Archive), **12** (© Swim Ink
2, LLC), **19** (© Nicole Duplaix), **21** (© Bettmann), **22** (©
Ursula Dueren/epa), **25** (© Lowell Georgia), **26** (© Christinne
Muschi/Reuters); Getty Images pp. **10** (Hulton Archive), **11**
(Hulton Archive), **13** (AFP), **14** (Jupiterimages/Workbook
Stock), **18** (Scott Wintrow), **29** (Hulton Archive); iStockphoto
p. **5** (© Peter Engelsted Jonasen); Courtesy of the Board of
Trustees, National Gallery of Art, Washington p. **8** (John
Bill Ricketts by Gilbert Stuart, Gift of Mrs. Robert B. Noyes
in memory of Elisa Riggs, Image Courtesy of the Board of
Trustees, National Gallery of Art, Washington); Photolibrary
p. **9** (The National Archives/Imagestate); Rex Features p. **28**
(SNAP); Shutterstock pp. **16** (© Tatiana Morozova), **24** (©
PavleMarjanovic).

Cover photograph of an acrobat performing a flying aerial
chiffon during the World Acrobats Show, 2009 reproduced
with permission of Corbis (© Narong Sangnak/epa).

We would like to thank Sylvia Hernandez-DiStasi and Jackie
Murphy for their invaluable help in the preparation of this
book.

Every effort has been made to contact copyright holders of
material reproduced in this book. Any omissions will be
rectified in subsequent printings if notice is given to the
publisher.

## Author

Marc Nobleman is the author of
more than 70 books. He speaks
regularly to young people about the
joys, challenges, and methods of
writing books.

## Literacy consultant

Jackie Murphy is Director of Arts at
a centre of teaching and learning.
She works with teachers, artists,
and school leaders internationally.

## Expert

Sylvia Hernandez-DiStasi began
performing at the age of seven
with her family of acrobats, The
Hernandez Troupe. She currently
runs The Actors Gymnasium, a
circus and performing arts school.

# Contents

Some words are printed in bold, **like this**. You can find out what they mean by looking in the glossary on page 30.

# Step right up!

Outside a town, an enormous, colourful tent stands in a field. Inside are treats for children of all ages. See fierce animals and fearless **acrobats**! Smell sawdust and sweet candy floss! Hear upbeat music! Feel your sides ache from laughing at lovable clowns! The circus is here!

## What is a circus?

A circus is a **troupe** (group) of people and sometimes animals that performs dazzling entertainments for an audience. In various forms, circuses have been entertaining people worldwide since the days of ancient Rome. Today, some circuses blend traditions from around the world.

The word *circus* comes from the Latin word for *circle*. At first, circuses took place in a single circular area called a **ring**. To draw bigger crowds, circus owners added more **acts**, or performances. To fit those acts, they added additional rings. The three-ring circus became especially popular. Some circuses have as many as five rings.

The person who runs the show under the spotlight is the ringmaster.

Circuses in Europe did not begin using tents when American circuses did. They continued to put on shows in permanent structures.

## Different town each day

Traditional circuses travelled from village to village. They were held outdoors or in simple structures, so they did not perform in the winter.

A circus would set up at dawn, parade in the morning to draw a crowd, perform one or two shows, pack up after dark, and move to the next town overnight. Today some circuses stay in one permanent location.

For hundreds of years, for thousands of people, the most exciting day of the year has been when the circus comes to town.

### Circus travel

Early circuses travelled by wagons. In the 1800s, many began to use trains. In the 1900s, some circuses switched to lorries.

This illustration shows chariots racing in the Circus Maximus in ancient Rome.

# The circus through the centuries

Circuses date back at least as far as ancient Rome. The first and biggest circus in ancient Rome began around 50 BC in the Circus Maximus, an enormous stadium. **Spectators** were thrilled by events such as chariot races, **equestrian** (horse) **acts**, **acrobatics**, and wild-animal displays.

After the Roman Empire ended, hundreds of years passed before the term *circus* was commonly used again. However, people did continue to enjoy circus-type entertainment. In the Middle Ages, the period from roughly AD 500 to 1500, **acrobats** and animal trainers travelled throughout Europe performing at fairs and markets.

## Birth of the modern circus

A British former soldier called Philip Astley is often considered to be the father of the modern circus. In 1768 he began performing horse-riding stunts in London. In one of his tricks, he stood on a galloping horse with one foot on the horse's back and the other on the horse's head. Astley had worked out that riding around a **ring** of a certain size helped him keep his balance. He called this ring "the Circle".

Astley called his performance ring "the Circle".
Performing in a ring became a circus tradition.

Soon Astley added musicians and a clown called Mr Merryman to his performances. He also built Astley's Amphitheatre, a large, permanent hall in which to perform. Astley did not describe his show as a "circus". However, his nearby competitor, Charles Hughes, used the term for his own show, and it stuck.

## The circus spreads

In 1782 Astley opened a second circus in Paris. He went on to found a total of 19 circuses across Europe. Hughes brought his act to Russia.

## The circus in North America

Inspired by Astley and Hughes, a talented rider called John Bill Ricketts brought the circus to North America. His first US performance was in Philadelphia in 1793. It took place in an open-air structure that seated 800 spectators, which Ricketts built himself. It was a hit. Before Ricketts' circus was a month old, US President George Washington attended a performance.

Like Astley and Hughes, Ricketts started with equestrian acts and later added acrobatics and comedy. Ricketts also toured his show along the eastern United States and Canada.

## Growth of the circus

As circuses became popular, they developed different traditions. Travelling circuses usually performed in uncovered wooden structures. In Delaware, USA, in 1825, Joshuah Purdy Brown held his show under a large canvas tent.

John Bill Ricketts brought the circus to North America.

A **big top** (circus tent) meant the show could go on even in the rain. Also, tents were portable. Circuses no longer had to buy wood and build structures at each new site. Tents also allowed circuses to move faster. They could now perform in more cities – and make more money.

This poster **advertises** the circus at the 1886 World's Fair.

## Menageries

People had displayed exotic animals, including lions and polar bears, in North America by the middle of the 1700s. In 1832 Brown became the first person to add

### Star elephants

The first elephant in North America arrived in 1796 and later joined a circus. The second elephant in North America was called Old Bet. In the early 1800s, her owner charged people money to see her. He walked her from town to town at night so fewer people would get a glimpse for free.

# The greatest shows on earth

In the 1840s businessman P. T. Barnum became famous for running a museum of "**curiosities**" in New York City, USA. He was brilliant at drawing a crowd with rare **attractions** such as General Tom Thumb, a dwarf who sang, danced, and imitated famous people. Barnum also made up attractions such as a "mermaid mummy". The mummy was actually a dummy made from a monkey and a fish.

In 1871 Barnum and businessman W. C. Coup formed a circus that would also display Barnum's curiosities. The curiosities developed into a popular circus feature called a **sideshow**, which is a smaller attraction at a circus. They **advertised** their circus as "the Greatest Show on Earth".

In 1880 Barnum partnered with circus organizer James Bailey. They created a three-**ring extravaganza** that became known as the Barnum and Bailey Circus.

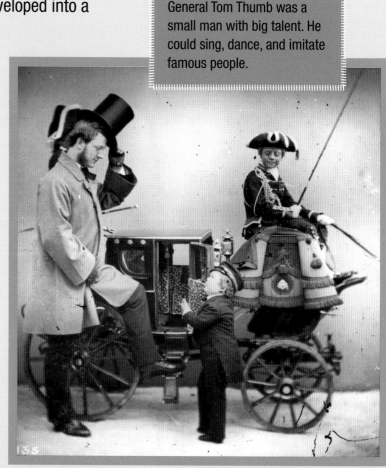

General Tom Thumb was a small man with big talent. He could sing, dance, and imitate famous people.

## A talented family

Meanwhile, in Wisconsin, five brothers called Ringling had grown up in awe of the circus. In 1884 they created their own. Each brother had a skill. One was good at advertising. Another was good at picking **acts**. Another handled the money. Together they were a success.

In 1919, by which time Barnum, Bailey, and more than half of the Ringling brothers had died, their circuses merged to become the Ringling Bros and Barnum & Bailey Circus. It is still one of the biggest names in circuses today.

## The circus goes wild

Beginning in the 1880s, William "Buffalo Bill" Cody toured a cowboy-**themed** circus called Buffalo Bill's Wild West. Acts included rodeo stunts, shooting competitions, and short plays about train robberies and bison hunting.

This poster advertises the Ringling Bros and Barnum & Bailey Circus as "the Greatest Show on Earth"..

# Thrilling acts

At the circus, audiences are often looking up. **Acrobats**, tight-rope walkers, and human cannonballs entertain audiences from above. While watching **aerial** (in the air) displays, some **spectators** "ooh" and "aah". Others hold their breath. Everyone hopes no one falls.

## Air acrobats

**Trapeze** artists perform in multiple ways. In static (not moving) trapeze, performers balance on and hang from trapezes (bars hung between two ropes) that stay in place. Swinging trapeze artists perform on moving trapezes. In flying trapeze, the flyer leaps from one trapeze and grabs another trapeze or a catcher on another trapeze. Flying **aerialists** work over a safety net.

VAN AMBURGH & CO'S

CANTON MAY 17

MENAGERIE, CIRCUS AND COLOSSEUM

In the earliest trapeze **acts**, performers leaped to and from bars connected to the ground.

## Daring young man

In 1859, the French aerialist Jules Léotard became the first known person to do a mid-air somersault while performing a flying trapeze act. He wore a skintight costume that is now called after him.

## Top of the big top

About 9 metres (30 feet) up, circus tightrope walkers cross a wire thinner than 2.5 centimetres (1 inch). Some carry a pole to help balance. On the wire, tightrope walkers do more than walk. Additional stunts include juggling and forming human pyramids. Some perform without a net. This makes the audience feel the act is more dangerous.

## Hanging by a thread

In *corde lisse* (French for "smooth rope"), an aerialist performs various hangs and other tricks on a **vertical** (up and down) rope. A similar act is the "Spanish web", in which aerialists also spin on the rope. Both acts require strength and grace.

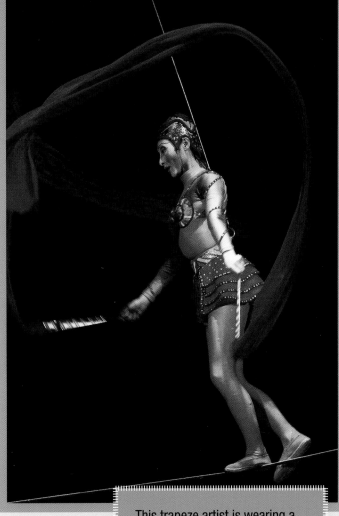

This trapeze artist is wearing a safety wire in case she falls.

### Boom!

Cannon acts offer thrills that are both high and fast. A person shot out of a cannon can travel 105 kilometres (65 miles) an hour.

# Unbelievable feats

Not all the circus thrills are on high. Amazing stunts also fill the **rings** below. Many acts wow spectators at the ground.

"Strongmen" and "strongwomen" were popular circus **attractions** in the 1800s. They bent metal bars in their hands and lifted heavy blocks of metal.

**Contortionists** bend their bodies into positions that do not seem humanly possible. Because of their training and flexibility, it is not painful, although it may look that way.

**Stilt** walkers balance high in the air as they walk on high poles, or stilts.

Fire breathers must be careful not to swallow the fuel or to let the fire reach their face.

Sword swallowers do not eat swords. They slide them far down their throat. It takes practice and concentration, but it remains very risky.

Fire breathers appear to shoot flames from their mouth. By spitting fuel such as kerosene over a flame in certain ways, they create fiery effects.

# Spin plates

Many circus skills would be fun to learn, but let's start with one that does not require a net!

Plate spinners spin plates on top of vertical sticks. The sticks are held or lined up in front of the performers. The performers must keep all the plates spinning at once.

## Steps to follow:

1. Find a straight stick or other wooden bar that is 0.5 or 1 metre (2 or 3 feet) long.

2. Get a heavy-duty paper or plastic plate.

3. In a clear area outside, place the plate on top of the stick and try to spin it.

4. Experiment with different methods. Should you keep your legs straight or bend them at the knees? Where should you look while you spin? Practise with a sibling or friend.

5. When you are both ready, compete to see who can keep a plate spinning longer.

Practise plate-spinning before you compete with your friends to see who can spin the longest.

# Circus favourites

People go to the circus to gasp, but also to laugh. The **comic relief** of a circus is the clowns. Many clowns do not speak during performances. Certain clown routines have become classics, such as the small car that somehow holds many clowns.

## Clown categories

There are several kinds of clowns. "Whiteface clowns" commonly wear white make-up and small, pointed hats. Their clothes can be either baggy or fitted and usually match. When performing with other clowns, a whiteface clown often plays the "boss".

"Auguste clowns" commonly wear bright wigs, mismatched clothes, and floppy shoes. Their faces often feature big red noses and outlined mouths. Much of their humour is **slapstick**, such as falling and chasing.

"Character clowns" come in different varieties, such as the tramp or the police officer. They often perform alone.

Some clowns do more than make an audience laugh. This auguste clown performs **acrobatics** as well.

Some modern clowns do not wear wild make-up or costumes. They sometimes interact with the audience, even asking for volunteers.

# Design a clown costume

Create a new, modern clown look for the 2010s.

**Steps to follow:**

1. Look at pictures of existing clown types online or in books. Look at the range of different costumes and make-up. Make a mental note of what you like and do not like about each.

2. Choose an idea for your clown. Do you want him or her to be punk, formal, tropical, robotic, or something else?

3. Sketch two designs based on your idea. You may use elements from existing clowns, but most of your design should be new. Think about clothing, make-up design, and what will be funny!

4. Decide which of your designs you like better. Ink and colour that design.

5. Name your new type of clown. Display your new clown for friends and family to see.

What will your new clown look like? Will any of its features remind you of yourself.

Circuses save the biggest animal acts for last. Elephants often perform after the big cats.

## Circus animals

Some of the most popular circus stars are furry and four-legged. Animals including horses, elephants, lions, and bears have appeared in circuses. Some animal **acts** perform in an unexpected way. For example, elephants stand on their hind legs and walk in a row. Other animal acts impress audiences because of the danger involved. Trainers have walked into the cages of growling big cats.

## Celebrity circus creatures

Two of the biggest circus stars were big themselves. In 1882 Barnum introduced Jumbo, a 6.4-tonne, 3.7-metre- (12-foot-) tall elephant. As a **publicity** stunt, Barnum got Jumbo to lead an elephant parade across the Brooklyn Bridge in New York. Now the word *jumbo* means "enormous".

Debuting in 1938, Gargantua (which means "large") was a gorilla with a scarred face. His frightening look made him popular, and his popularity saved the Ringling Brothers circus from going out of business.

## Against their will

While the use of animals in circuses is a beloved tradition, it also causes concern. Some people claim that the training is abusive, and that the animals perform out of fear. Investigators have seen trainers strike elephants with whips and hooks. Some stunts put animals in danger, such as when a tiger jumps through a fire hoop. But circuses and trainers claim animals are treated with love and are well cared for. Animal rights organizations are working to free circus animals. Some countries ban animals from circuses, and some circuses choose to have no animals.

### Flea circus

In the 1800s and 1900s, flea circuses were popular **sideshow attractions**. Real fleas were attached to tiny bicycles or chariots. **Spectators** looked through special lenses to watch the fleas "perform". A flea circus has a limited audience — only the number of people who can crowd around a small table. To earn more money, flea circus managers would run dozens of 10-minute shows a day.

Two fleas attached to carts race during this miniature circus.

# The dark side of circuses

Circuses bring great joy, but they have also been places of cruelty and tragedy. Many circuses have taken advantage of people who are different from others. Other times, tragedy has struck during circuses.

## The shame of circuses past

Some circuses used to include "freak shows". They featured people with unusual talents, such as sword swallowers, and those who looked different, such as people with many tattoos. They also included people who looked different but not by choice, such as bearded women and so-called "Siamese twins", or conjoined (attached) twins. Some of these people were forced to appear in freak shows, but others wanted to join.

Throughout the 1900s, more and more people felt that freak shows unkindly took advantage of some people. Circuses stopped including freak shows. Now it is no longer acceptable to display a person as a "freak".

## The Connecticut fire

On 6 July 1944, disaster struck a circus in Hartford in the state of Connecticut, USA. To stop a leak in the tent, the circus had waterproofed it. Tragically, they used substances that burn easily, including petrol.

Twenty minutes into the show, the tent caught fire. The band began to play "Stars and Stripes Forever". At the circus, that song is played only during emergencies. It alerts the performers that there is danger and is meant to calm the audience as they exit. Yet that day, the music did not help.

Spectators run for their lives during the Hartford circus fire of 1944.

Almost 7,000 **spectators** were in attendance. Some did not realize they could have escaped under the tent flaps. Instead they rushed to where they had entered, but animal equipment now blocked the way. The tent burned to ashes in six minutes. Hundreds were injured, and 168 people died.

## A sad statistic

In terms of lives lost, the Hartford fire was the worst circus disaster in history.

# Learning circus skills

Today, anybody – both children and adults – can learn how to participate in a circus. They go to circus schools or camps for young people.

## Circus schools

Special schools worldwide teach circus skills. **Trapeze** schools give everyday people the chance to feel the rush of an **aerial act**. Circus schools across the country offer skills workshops and courses for adults and children.

Through the Mobile Mini Circus for Children in Afghanistan, children create and perform their own circus. In Australia an organization called Cirkidz trains people as young as two-and-a-half in the circus arts.

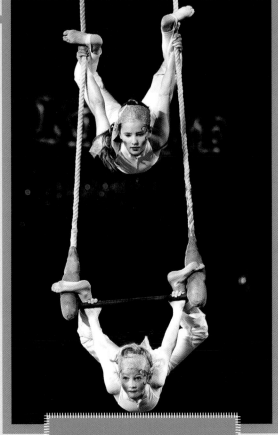

Children **acrobats** perform on a trapeze at this circus in Munich, Germany.

## Youth circuses and camps

Circus Smirkus is an international youth circus and camp based in Vermont, USA. Its performers are between 10 and 18 years old. Every summer it introduces a new story line and goes on tour, doing 70 shows in two months. Circus camps can also be found in countries such as the United Kingdom and Germany.

# Write circus lyrics

"Thunder and Blazes", composed by Louis-Philippe Laurendeau, based on "Entrance of the Gladiators" by Julius Fucík is a famous circus march. But it had no words to sing along to ... until now.

**Steps to follow:**

1. Listen to "Thunder and Blazes" online or on a CD. (You will recognize it!) How does the music make you feel?

2. Think of how the music reminds you of the circus. Does it remind you of acrobats, animals, or something else from the circus? Write lyrics (words) to fit the music. Make the words describe a circus adventure!

3. Perform your new mix for family and friends. If you do not want to sing alone, first teach it to a sibling or friend.

When writing lyrics to "Thunder and Blazes", think about how the music makes you feel.

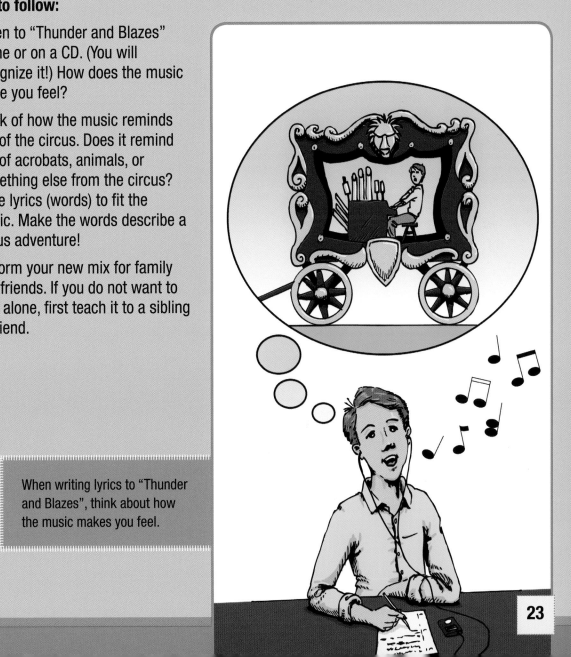

# Reinventing the circus

Two hundred years ago, a circus was often a town's only entertainment for the whole year. Today, circuses compete every day against films, concerts, theatre, sports, games, reading, television, and the Internet for people's time and money.

## An international feel

While circuses still entertain with upbeat music, clueless clowns, and spine-tingling **acts**, they have updated these features for modern audiences. Many circuses today bring in performers, acts, and customs from around the world.

## Telling a story

Circuses used to be a series of unrelated acts. Today some circuses tell a story and have a **theme** (central idea). In some recent circuses, there are no animal performers. The music is new and created specifically for that circus. The performance is in a theatre, not a tent. Some use modern machines such as motorcycles. This style of circus is called "*cirque nouveau*", which is French for "new circus".

Members of the Great Chinese Circus perform during their tour throughout Europe.

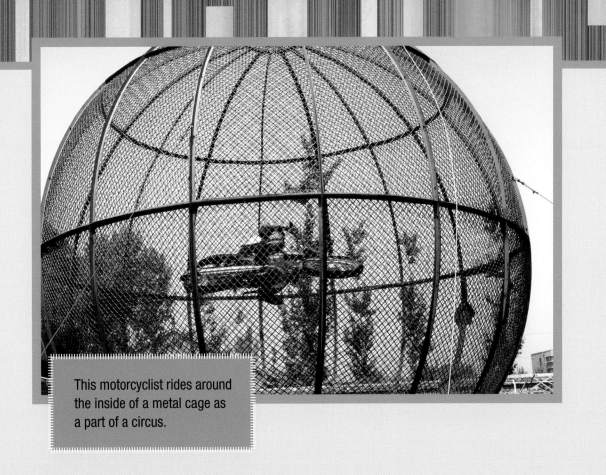

This motorcyclist rides around the inside of a metal cage as a part of a circus.

## Traditional circuses keep up

In response to successful new circuses, the long-running Ringling Bros and Barnum & Bailey Circus tried a new kind of show in 2006. It was the first major change the circus had made in 50 years.

The three **rings** and big cats were gone, but the circus added a running story about a present-day family that dreams of joining the circus. It also added a jumbo video screen to show story flashbacks and instant replays.

### Biggest big top

As of 2009 the largest permanent **big top** in the world is at Circus Circus, a hotel in Las Vegas, USA. In 1997 it changed from being traditional to being a more modern kind of circus.

# Circus Oz

Circus Oz premiered in Australia in 1978 and has since performed in dozens of countries. Some circuses have a large cast, but each Circus Oz show features only 11 to 13 performers. Each performer has multiple skills, from **acrobatics** to clowning. Circus Oz uses a wide range of elements, including rock and roll and humour.

In the Cirque du Soleil production of *Ovo*, the performers play insects who discover a strange egg.

# Cirque du Soleil

Founded in Québec, Canada, Cirque du Soleil (meaning "Circus of the Sun" in French) began in 1984. This circus company produces multiple shows at once, each with its own theme. Some shows stay in one location, while others tour the world.

Cirque du Soleil's experiments go beyond new stories and music. One Cirque du Soleil show, *O*, features underwater acrobatics performed in a giant tank. Another show, *KÀ*, doesn't use a traditional stage. Instead the action takes place on large, moveable platforms.

# Circus Amok

In New York City parks, Circus Amok puts on free circuses with jugglers, **stilt** walkers, and life-sized puppets. Founded by bearded woman Jennifer Miller, Circus Amok's message is the importance of being true to yourself and fair to others.

# "Dark" circuses

Some new circuses combine circus **acts** with street performance, comedy, and electronic music. Other groups feature comedy and rap music to appeal to younger audiences. Modern circuses can also have a creepy side to them, unlike traditional circuses.

## Familiar faces

Some circuses include characters created in other types of entertainment. For example, the Cole Bros Circus has acts featuring Spider-Man and the Hulk.

# Beyond the big top

The **acts** are death-defying. The music is delightful. The peanuts are delicious! These are only three reasons why the circus remains a beloved form of entertainment.

## Circus in print

People have written stories about the circus for all ages. A 2000 novel by Darren Shan called *Cirque du Freak* is about vampires and a circus out of a nightmare. In the Batman series of comics and films, Batman's partner, Robin, was born into a family of circus **aerialists** called the Flying Graysons.

## Circus on screen

The animated film *Dumbo* (1941) is about a lovable circus elephant able to do something Jumbo never could: use his big ears to fly. In 1953 the Academy Award for Best Picture went to *The Greatest Show on Earth*. The film takes place at a Ringling Bros and Barnum & Bailey Circus and features many real performers.

Dumbo is one circus star who continues to entertain decades after his debut.

## Circus in song

The circus has inspired much music. The 1867 song "The Daring Young Man on the Flying **Trapeze**" is about Jules Léotard (see page 12). Ever since the 1950s in the United Kingdom, the song "Nellie the Elephant" has enchanted children.

## The circus is everywhere

In popular culture, clowns often appear outside the circus. Bozo the Clown shot to fame on television in the 1950s. The clown Ronald McDonald is the mascot of the McDonald's fast food chain.

The common phrase "run away and join the circus" suggests that the circus may just be the most fun place one can imagine. Many children *do* want to run to the circus – but usually simply to watch it!

Bozo, an auguste clown, has been portrayed by hundreds of performers.

## One more circus

The word *circus* also describes an out-of-control situation. In a loud, crowded shop, you might say, "It's a circus in here."

# Glossary

**acrobat** person who entertains people by performing physical feats that require a lot of strength and skill

**acrobatic** describes a gymnastic feat that requires a lot of skill and strength

**act** circus performance

**advertise** announce an upcoming performance to try to interest people in coming

**aerial** in the air

**aerialist** person who performs feats in the air, such as a trapeze artist

**attraction** interesting performance or display at a circus

**comic relief** something that provides humour

**contortionist** person who bends his or her body into extreme positions to entertain others

**curiosity** something a person wants to learn more about

**equestrian** on horseback

**extravaganza** wonderful entertainment event

**menagerie** group of wild animals on display

**publicity** action taken to tell people about something that is for sale

**ring** circular area in which a circus act performs

**sideshow** smaller attraction at a circus

**slapstick** physical humour such as falling over, chasing something, or bumping into something

**spectator** person who watches a performance

**stilt** special pole that performers walk on, making them appear taller

**theme** idea that a story is about

**trapeze** bar hung between two ropes and used in aerial circus acts

**troupe** group of performers

**vertical** up and down

# Find out more

## Books

*The Great and Only Barnum: The Tremendous, Stupendous Life of Showman P. T. Barnum*, Candace Fleming (Schwartz & Wade, 2009)

*Would You Believe … a Circus Horse Could Count?!*, Richard Platt (OUP, 2009)

## Websites

The Circus Space
www.thecircusspace.co.uk/index.htm
This circus school in London has special courses for children and young people to learn circus skills.

Circus Schools
www.circusarts.org.uk/i-want-to/learn-circus-skills/youth-circus-workshop-database.php
If you are interested in learning circus skills then have a look at this web page to find a circus school near you.

## Places to visit

Chinese State Circus
www.chinesestatecircus.com
This circus has multiple locations in England. Visit the website for schedules.

Blackpool Tower and Circus
The Promenade
Blackpool FY1 4BJ
www.theblackpooltower.co.uk/index.php
This circus is based in one location and there are many other activities to enjoy at the Tower.

# Index